How schools teach reading

Angela Redfern & Viv Edwards

Reading & Language Information Centre, University of Reading

WHSMITH
EXCLUSIVE
·BOOKS·

© 1992 Angela Redfern and Viv Edwards
Published by the Reading and Language
Information Centre, University of
Reading
ISBN 0704905477
Photographs by Dave Andrews,
Gary Harman, David Hinder and
Tony Rose
Designed by The Design Works, Reading
Typeset by Page One, Reading
Printed and bound in Great Britain by
Radavian Press, Reading

Contents

Acknowledgements

Warm thanks to the children, parents and teachers at Redlands Primary School, Reading for their permission to take the photographs used throughout this book.

Extracts from the following books have been used with the kind permission of the publishers, authors and illustrators: *Terrible, Terrible Tiger* © Colin and Jackie Hawkins, published in the UK by Walker Books Ltd; *Doing the Washing* © Sarah Garland, first published in the UK by The Bodley Head; *Through my Window* © Tony Bradman and Eileen Browne, published by Methuen, London; and *My Favourite Things* © Jennie Ingham and Prodeepta Das, published by Jennie Ingham Associates; *English in the National Curriculum* pp7–8 © 1990 HMSO.

What parents want to know about reading

The way schools teach reading has changed a great deal in recent years. The approaches and materials we see in classrooms today are very different from the ones that teachers used when we were children. Reading is very important to a child's success in school and it is natural that parents should want to find out more. This book attempts to answer the questions that they often ask:

- Are reading standards really falling?
- What methods do schools use to teach reading?
- What kinds of materials do teachers use?
- How do teachers encourage the reading habit?
- How do teachers assess progress in reading?
- What do you do if you think your child has a problem?
- How can parents help?

Reading is very important to a child's success in school and it is natural that parents should want to find out more

The reading crisis?

A look at the evidence and how the media distort the true picture

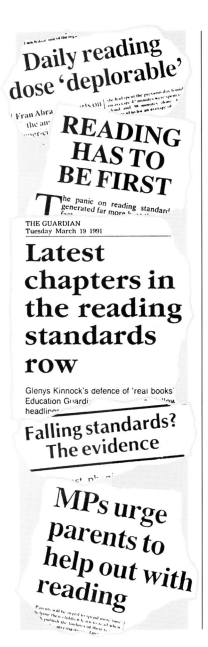

Reading hit the headlines in the 1990s with a series of sensationalist claims that standards were falling. Accusations about the failure of so-called 'caring' teachers and their 'trendy' or 'cranky' teaching methods gathered momentum. The verdict of the popular press was that teachers and teacher trainers were to blame for the drop in standards.

Concern about falling standards is nothing new. Complaints about children's standards in reading can be traced back for over a hundred years. So to what extent is the present hue and cry about reading based on facts? Is there really a reading crisis?

The evidence

Two major inquiries have challenged claims of falling standards. Her Majesty's Inspectors (HMI) carried out a large-scale inspection of reading in primary schools in 1990. They visited 470 classes in 120 schools and heard 2,000 children read aloud, but found no evidence that standards had fallen since the last major survey of primary education in 1978. Reading standards were high in 30 per cent of schools and satisfactory in a further 50 per cent.

The second inquiry took the form of a Parliamentary Select Committee, set up in 1990 to examine the teaching of reading in primary schools. After considering evidence from a very wide range of witnesses, the Select Committee found that claims of falling standards had *not* been proved.

Not everyone agrees. Studies in a number of local education authorities have pointed to a decline in reading standards. A national sample survey published at the end of 1991 suggested that the reading standards of seven and eight year olds had declined by between three and five months since 1987.

Possible explanations

But even if we accept that there has been a fall in reading standards, there is no conclusive explanation as to why this should have happened. The press and politicians have been quick to point the finger at modern methods of teaching reading. However, it is difficult to see how this could be the case, since most schools use a mixture of methods.

So what else could account for the apparent decline? Many teachers feel that the demands of the National Curriculum have made it impossible to spend as much time on teaching reading. A recently published survey of international reading standards adds weight to this claim. In New Zealand, which is reputed to have the highest levels of literacy, half of every day is spent on reading and writing activities.

Other people have pointed to the fact that the sharpest falls in reading standards have been observed in the more disadvantaged schools. They argue that we should pay more attention to the effects of poverty on children's education.

A nation of illiterates?

Unfortunately, emotion plays a bigger part than reason in the debate on reading standards. This was clearly shown by reactions to the results of the first national tests for seven year olds (SATS) when 28 per cent of children failed to reach Level 2, the standard expected of the average child of this age. Many people interpreted this to mean that more than a quarter of seven year olds could not read at all.

A closer look at the facts suggests that press and politicians seriously over-reacted. Many teachers have questioned the level of difficulty of the books which were chosen for the tests. They argue that some of the books included in Level 2 should in fact have been placed at Level 3.

But even if we put to one side the choice of books, there is no reason to suggest that so many seven year olds simply cannot read. It is likely that as many as 10 per cent of the children achieving Level 1 were able to read with some fluency but fell down on just one or two of the Level 2 requirements. For instance, they may not have been able to use a dictionary.

It is also important to remember that children learn at different rates and that some seven year olds will not yet have 'taken off' in reading. As many as 15 per cent of children achieving Level 1 will have learning difficulties or do not speak English as their first language.

The details of what is happening to reading in schools risk being lost in political arguments which make selective use of the facts. None the less, no one disagrees that there is a fundamental need to teach *all* children to read fluently and with understanding.

Methods of teaching reading

A look at the pros and cons of the different ways of teaching reading

The 1990 HMI report on reading found that the vast majority of schools use a mixture of methods to teach reading. They are well aware that no one approach works well for every child. The English National Curriculum document also favours a mixture of methods. It would seem that there is a good deal more agreement about the teaching of reading than the popular press suggests.

What happens when we read?

For a long time teachers thought that learning to read was a purely mechanical process and that children simply needed to learn how to crack the code of written symbols by building up a set of skills in strict order. The two most widely used teaching methods to grow out of this view of reading are **look and say** and **phonics.**

From the 1960s onwards, researchers began to question ideas of this kind. By observing closely what children actually do when they read aloud and analysing the mistakes they make, it became clear that reading is far more than simply 'cracking the code'. In order to make sense of print, we make intelligent guesses. We use our experience of language and life, and our knowledge of the way that stories work to help us. The **language experience** approach to the teaching of reading has grown out of this

Children may not always read exactly what is written on the page, but they use their knowledge of language and books to make intelligent guesses

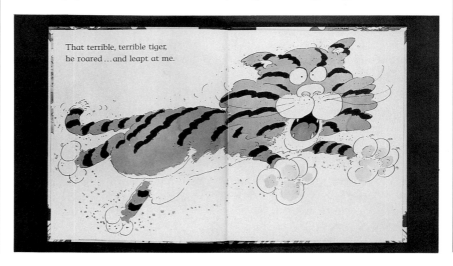

That terrible, terrible tiger, he roared...and leapt at me.

more recent understanding of what happens when we read.

When faced with the pages shown opposite, an inexperienced reader might well read, 'The terrible, terrible tiger, he roared ... and jumped on me.'

Although this is not accurate, the child would be showing that she knows the story must make sense, and she would be using the picture and her own knowledge of language to do just that. This is an intelligent reading strategy. As long as her mistake or 'miscue' does not change the meaning, she should not be corrected. As she becomes more experienced, this kind of miscue will gradually disappear.

Children can often make sense of stories on their own...

and with their friends

The look and say method teaches children to recognise whole words

Look and say method

This method relies on teaching children to recognise individual words. Flashcards are practised daily in class and are often taken home in little tins for extra practice. In this way, children develop a growing vocabulary of key words they recognise on sight. Failed words go back into the tin for further practice.

Once children can recognise the first set of words, they are given their first book to read. This contains only the words they already know so that their early attempts at reading are sure to be a success.

Concerns
- Children with a poor visual memory find this method difficult.
- Repetition can be tedious.
- Books with a limited number of words can sound very stilted.
- Children have no strategies to help them read words they have not met.

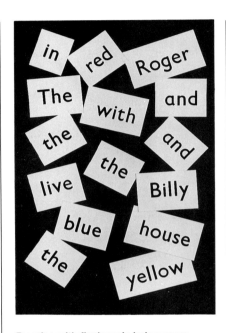

Practice with flashcards helps some children but not all

Phonic method

While still concerned with 'cracking the code', this method concentrates not on words but on even smaller units: letters and their sounds.

Children are introduced to single sounds at the beginning of words (e.g. *p, t, s*), to blends (e.g. *br, pr, sl*), to clusters (e.g. *spr, str*), to digraphs (e.g. *ch, th, sh*), to the last letters in words (e.g. sto*p*), and so on. Very often they practise letter and sound recognition through activities such as filling in missing letters, circling words and mapping objects to initial letters.

Concerns

- The relationship between sounds and letters is not always straightforward (e.g. eye, pie, high, cry).
- Our ability to distinguish between sounds develops at different rates. Boys tend to develop later than girls.
- Children with poor auditory discrimination find this method difficult.
- Children with ear, nose and throat problems may find themselves at a disadvantage, especially in winter.
- Regional variations such as 'fick' for 'thick' or 'bruvver' for 'brother' can lead to confusion.

The phonic method concentrates on letters and their sounds

Children do exercises to practise matching letters with sounds

The language experience method emphasises meaning from the start

Language experience method

The language experience method developed in response to more recent information on how we read. Children dictate their story to the teacher who then writes it down. This process helps children to see the link between talking, reading and writing. They are highly motivated because the story is their own. This helps them to remember the words and ensures that their early attempts at reading are a success. Meaning is emphasised from the start.

The best known commercial example of this method is *Breakthrough to Literacy*. 120 of the words most commonly used by children are printed on individual cards and displayed on a large board. Finding and replacing the words on the board helps draw children's attention to word shapes.

With the teacher's help, children compose a 'story' about their own experiences by placing the word cards in a special stand. The teacher writes the finished stories in the children's books for them to illustrate.

When children can recognise about 20 words, they are given their own folder, a smaller version of the big board. Later, when they know virtually all the Breakthrough words on sight, they move on to their own personal dictionaries, set out in alphabetical order. Teachers write down the words children need for them to copy into their story books.

Concerns
- Many teachers find Breakthrough very 'fiddly'. They require good organisational skills if they are to use it to best effect.
- Some children find it difficult to manipulate the tiny word cards.
- Some children find it tedious to copy out their story after they have composed it in the stand.

Children use words from a folder to create their own stories

The apprenticeship method emphasises enjoyment and involvement in the story

Apprenticeship method

We are surrounded by the written word. Writing rolls across TV screens and reading material floats through letter boxes. People read and write cards and letters, and fill in forms. By the time they arrive in school, most children will have realised that marks on paper are a way of communicating a message.

The **appenticeship** method builds both on this experience of print, and on the knowledge of stories, language and life which children bring with them to school. The emphasis is on enjoying books, responding to the story and comparing it with their own experience. Children regularly read a book alongside the teacher until they feel ready to take over on their own.

Many myths have grown up around the apprenticeship method. It is accused of offering no structure and of leaving children to learn to read as if by magic in a room full of books. In reality, schools that choose children's books rather than reading schemes usually have a well-planned programme for teaching the full range of strategies that children need to become fluent readers.

The apprenticeship method is sometimes mistakenly called the 'real books' method because of the great importance which it attaches to the quality of the books which children read.

In the early stages, teacher and child read the book together

Much ado about nothing?

Many people have tried to blame falling reading standards on the introduction of modern teaching methods. There would seem to be no justification for this view. The 1990 HMI report on reading points out that as few as 5 per cent of schools rely on just one teaching method. It also points out that reading standards are least satisfactory in schools which rely on a single approach – whether 'real books' or phonics.

The HMI, the National Curriculum Council and the vast majority of schools and teachers are agreed that if children are to become fluent readers:

- they should be encouraged to use their knowledge of life, language and their experience with books
- they need to build up a sight vocabulary
- they need to understand the link between letter sounds and symbols.

Part of the teacher's skill is to recognise the wide range of differences between children and to offer each child the right kind of support at the right time.

Parents can . . .
find out about a school's approach to teaching reading by:
- reading school brochures
- talking to the head teacher or, if the child is already at school, the class teacher
- attending meetings which the school may arrange for new parents
- attending curriculum evenings.

Nearly all schools use a mixture of methods to teach reading

The teachers must be able to respond to children's needs in different ways

Resources for reading

Making decisions about which books to buy and how to organise them in the classroom

Children need the experience of reading many different kinds of books

Teachers need to ensure that children are exposed to many different kinds of books – picture books, poetry, fiction and information. They have a responsibility for helping children think critically about what they read. They need to decide whether to use specially designed reading schemes, 'real books' or a mixture of the two. They also need to think of the most effective ways of using the very wide range of books aimed at young children learning to read.

Reading schemes

These are sets of 'reading books' especially written for the purpose of teaching children to read.

Reading schemes have several things in common:
- books are graded according to difficulty and have to be read in the correct sequence
- the vocabulary in the early stages is stilted and repetitious
- the storyline is often weak
- there is often competition among children to get to the end of the scheme first.

Originally, reading schemes were tied to a particular teaching method. For instance, *Ladybird* books and *One, Two, Three and Away* were published to support look and say methods, *Bangers and Mash* and *New Way* are based on phonics.

Several new schemes such as the *Longman Reading World*, the *Oxford Reading Tree* and *Sunshine Books* which have appeared on the market more recently take into account the new understanding of the reading process. There is a definite attempt to tell a story, to use more natural language and to appeal to children's sense of humour. Illustrations are also more colourful and attractive than in the older schemes. However, these more recent schemes still sometimes fail to excite children's imagination in the earliest stages.

Individualised reading

In the mid-1970s, the dissatisfaction which many people felt about the artificial language and weak story lines in reading schemes gave rise to a new method of organising reading materials, which has come to be known as **individualised reading** or **colour coding.**

A wide range of reading schemes, non-fiction books, poetry and stories are grouped into thirteen different reading levels. The 1990 HMI report on reading highlighted the fact that nearly all the schools where the teaching of reading was average or above average used this kind of grading system.

Individualised reading is used in a number of different ways. For instance, some schools keep a core reading scheme alongside other books at the same level; some schools give children a free hand in choosing what they want to read from a given level; others allow children to choose from a range of levels.

Schools using individualised reading still expect children to progress through the different stages, and this can give rise to competitiveness. However, children have access to a far wider range of books, writing styles and subject matter at any one level.

Reading schemes, non-fiction books, poetry and stories are grouped into thirteen different reading levels

Individualised reading allows children to choose from a wide range of books at a level they can read independently

All the books listed by the National Curriculum Council for the testing of seven year olds are 'real books'

'Real books'

The apprenticeship approach to the teaching of reading described on page 10 is sometimes mistakenly referred to as the 'real books' approach. 'Real books' is quite simply a term used to refer to books on sale at any book shop, rather than ones which have been specially written to teach children how to read. All the books listed by the National Curriculum Council as suitable for the testing of seven year olds, for instance, are 'real books'.

Teachers who use 'real books' need to decide whether children should be given a free choice or whether they should organise the books in different levels of difficulty.

Bias in books

Teachers need to provide children with a wide range of reading materials but they also need to look closely at the reading material which they offer. Some books present a view of the world which increases our understanding of other people and helps us to value and respect them. Others encourage us to see some groups of people as less important than others.

The vast majority of children's books are about white, middle class, able-bodied people living in an idealised world. Even when characters from minority groups, such as black people, women or the disabled, do appear in books, they are usually presented as spectators rather than active participants.

Many writers are trapped into portraying stereotypes. For instance, Afro-Caribbean children are presented as good at sports and music; Chinese families always work in a take-away; girls are home-loving, obedient and unadventurous. Some books are simply insulting: black people are presented as cannibals or savages; traditional 'female' qualities and working class accents and customs are ridiculed.

The National Curriculum English document makes it clear that teachers have a responsibility to find books that offer a wider world view:

> "Texts need to reflect the multicultural nature of society, including home language and dual language texts, both in fiction and in non-fiction . . . Care should be taken to ensure that all these materials and their use reflect the equal opportunities policy of the school and the local education authority."

Parents can . . .
- choose books which present different cultural and social groups in positive ways (see details on the Letterbox Library on page 42)
- discuss with their children any reservations they may have about books which present minorities in a negative way.

Most children's books are about white, middle-class, able-bodied people living in an idealised world

Teachers have a responsibility to find books that offer a wider world view

Reading in action

A closer look at how schools promote the reading habit and help children to become fluent readers

There is a strong emphasis in schools today on making reading an enjoyable experience for children. Teachers attach a great deal of importance to providing:

- a well-stocked library
- attractive displays of books and children's writing
- inviting book corners
- listening corners with a good supply of taped stories, rhymes and songs
- a school bookshop or book club
- visits from authors and illustrators
- visits to libraries and book fairs.

All these things help to make children feel valued members of what one writer has called 'the literacy club'.

A good attitude towards reading is essential, but is not enough in itself. Children must also have a wide exposure to print and plenty of opportunities to practise the strategies they need for fluent reading. Many other classroom activities help children to become competent readers, including:

- storytime
- hearing children read
- regular sessions where the whole class reads silently
- paired reading
- group reading
- games which help children focus on the details of print
- 'publishing' children's stories.

Storytime

Reading to children at least once a day is a standard feature of primary school classrooms – and with good reason. A vast amount of learning takes place when children listen to adults reading, which stands them in good stead when they read independently.

Parents can . . .

- enjoy nursery rhymes and songs with children to develop a sense of rhythm and rhyme
- share events of the day to develop skills of recalling, retelling and sequencing
- find a few minutes to read and talk about a book or chapter together
- ask children about the day's story in school.

A vast amount of learning takes place when children listen to adults reading

---

Stories enable children to . . .

- make sense of their own experiences

- project themselves into unfamiliar places, times, cultures

- gain sympathetic under standing of other ways of life

- broaden and deepen their imaginative experiences

- learn how narrative is structured

- predict outcomes

- respond critically to text

- engage emotionally with stories

- increase their vocabulary about books, e.g. title, chapter, etc

- pick up concepts about print, e.g. left to right, top to bottom

- increase their store of literary language

- savour the rhymes and rhythms of language

- widen their vocabulary.

Young children used to stand at the teacher's desk and try to read a short passage with complete accuracy

Becoming a fluent reader

Many teachers are convinced that by far the most important aspect of teaching reading is for an adult and child to spend time regularly sharing a book – 'hearing reading' as it is often called, or 'having a reading conference' as it is increasingly known.

For many years, the most common practice was for children to stand at the teacher's desk where they would try to read a short passage with complete accuracy. This rather mechanical exercise fitted in well with the 'cracking the code' approach to reading.

Today teachers realise the importance of making this a very special time that children can look forward to and enjoy. The idea is to read the whole of a short book or a chapter from a longer book, so that children can predict what may happen next while reading and appreciate the story as a whole. This approach is better suited to the view that successful readers go for meaning rather than simply decoding the written word.

The frequency of conferences depends on the skill and confidence of the reader. Many teachers find it helpful to arrange conferences for inexperienced readers two or three times a week, once a week for experienced younger readers and perhaps once a fortnight for experienced older readers.

These conferences provide teachers with a chance to help children develop useful reading strategies. The emphasis will change according to each child's needs and achievements.

The most important aspect of teaching reading is for an adult and child to spend time regularly sharing a book

Getting started

In the very beginning, it is likely that the child will listen while the teacher reads the words. Together, they will look at the illustrations and comment on what is happening.

At this early stage many children are happy to retell a well-loved story in their own words, turning the pages but paying little or no attention to the printed words. Teachers can encourage them to look at the print by running their finger along the line.

As experience with books grows, children often start to join in with phrases they remember. Stories and poems written in rhyme are excellent for encouraging this. Sometimes the teacher will stop before the end of the line and allow the child to take over.

First the child listens while the teacher reads the words

Hang up the socks.

Teachers encourage children to predict what mum will hang up next

Moving along

Teachers can 'warm up' the child by reading the title, looking at the cover and briefly chatting about what they might find inside. At the bottom of each page, they might also encourage the child to predict what will happen next. For instance, when looking at the pages above, from Sarah Garland's book, *Doing the Washing*, the teacher and child might talk about what the mother is going to hang up next, then turn over the page to see if they were right.

All sorts of discussion can grow out of sharing the book. What happened in the story? How does this compare with events in real life? Or with other stories they have read? Did they think the book was funny? Did they spot any interesting words and phrases?

Gathering momentum

As children build up their sight vocabulary and their knowledge of initial letters, teachers offer support in a variety of ways. The conference will begin as usual with a 'warm-up'. If a child misreads a word which does not alter the meaning, e.g. 'dad' for 'father', the teacher will accept it. Similarly if they hesitate, repeat a word or leave one out, the teacher will say nothing, provided that the meaning is not lost.

But what happens when children read a word which does change the meaning, or if they simply cannot read a word? The teacher can help by:

- pointing to the picture if it is relevant
- asking a question to remind them of the context, e.g. "Where did they say they were going?"
- re-reading the sentence with expression up to the unknown word to remind them of the context
- saying or pointing to the first letter of the word
- covering part of the word to make it easier to recognise
- telling the child the word to avoid losing momentum.

Again, the conference finishes with a discussion of what they have been reading.

Experienced readers

Once children want to read 'in their heads', it is unwise to slow them down by insisting on too much reading aloud. Maybe they will choose a favourite passage to share with the teacher, but the bulk of the conference will be spent:

- discussing the books they have read in some detail
- talking about the style of the author and the illustrator
- deciding whether to write a review, make a poster or share what they have read in some other way
- selecting what to read next.

> **Parents can ...**
> - share books appropriate for their children's level of development
> - praise their children's achievements
> - carry on reading aloud to their children, even when they have begun to read independently.

It is unwise to slow experienced readers down by insisting on too much reading aloud

Teachers encourage experienced readers to discuss the books they have read

*In many schools,
silent reading is
timetabled for up to
half an hour every
day*

The teacher reads her own book
alongside the children

USSR or ERIC

In many schools, USSR (uninterrupted, sustained, silent reading) or ERIC (everyone reading in class) is timetabled for up to half an hour every day, depending on the age of the children. Teachers act as models for the children and read their own book at the same time as the rest of the class. These sessions can be invaluable for two reasons:

• they teach children how to go about selecting a book. The teacher can make suggestions about favourite authors or favourite subjects. They can direct children to look at the 'blurb' to whet their appetites. They can encourage children to try out the first page for level of difficulty

• they help children develop a love of books. Teachers set the tone by sharing their enthusiasm for their own books, by showing real interest in the children's choices and by talking to them about what they have read at the end of the session.

> **Parents can . . .**
> • set a good example by making sure their children see them reading at home
> • talk about their own favourite authors and the kinds of books they like best.

Paired reading

This term was first used to describe the one-to-one pairing of an adult with a child. The adult and child both read the book out loud together, with the child setting the pace. If the child feels able to read a little on her own, she can give a signal such as a knock on the table or a nudge. If she stumbles over a word, the adult tells her what it is and carries on reading until she signals that she is ready to go on alone again.

More recently, the term **paired reading** has been used to describe any pairing of a more experienced with a less experienced reader, including two children in the same class or an older child with a younger child.

Parents can . . .
- do paired reading at home. This scheme was originally designed for parent-child partnerships.

More experienced readers can be paired with less experienced partners

Paired reading can help children grow in confidence

Making books is an important influence in learning to read

'Big books' are ideal for sharing with a group of children

Publishing children's work

In recent years, language experience approaches have been extended to include regular 'publishing' of children's stories and topic work. Making books has become an important influence in learning to read. The security of seeing your own words in print, the comfort of working with a friend, the pleasure in demonstrating skills as an illustrator or designer and the pride in the finished product as it takes its place on the classroom bookshelf – all these are powerful factors in helping children become confident readers.

Group reading

In group reading copies of the same book are shared around a small group of children to read in unison, in silence or to read short passages in turn. Sharing views about the book brings added enjoyment and is highly motivating.

The pattern can be varied. Children can be encouraged to work in pairs or in groups of three; they can work with or without the teacher, and so on.

Group reading with 'big books' is becoming popular, especially with early readers or those experiencing difficulty. The very large print in these large format versions of popular children's books makes them ideal for sharing with groups of children.

There are lots of activities that encourage children to look closely at print

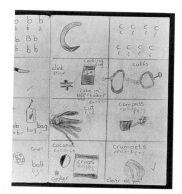

Activities for focusing on print

Children can be helped to focus on the details of the print, in a variety of ways:

- looking at print in the environment - food labels, shop signs, 'bus stop' 'exit' and so on
- comments when reading like "Oh, that's a long word isn't it?" or "What a tiny word, it's only got one letter!"
- games such as Snap, Matching Lotto, Spot the Difference, Pelmanism, What's Missing? and Kim's Game.

There are also many different games and activities to help children increase their phonic skills:

- I Spy, I went to Market, The Minister's Cat
- commercial games like Change a Letter or Scrabble
- computer games like Tray and Developing Tray
- alphabet songs
- picture dictionaries (above right)
- alliterative poems and stories (below right).

Parents can . . .
- enjoy all these activities at home with their children.

Reading to learn

Ways that teachers can help children to process new information

Children also need to read for information

Enjoying stories and poems is a central part of children's reading experience. However, they also need to read for information. You may remember spending a great deal of time in school copying out chunks of information from textbooks without remembering or even understanding much of it. Recent research has helped teachers to find more effective ways of guiding children through the various stages of processing information.

In working together on a class topic, groups of children are likely to go through the following stages:

- listing what they already know
- formulating questions about what they need to find out
- locating information in the library
- selecting the information they need from books
- organising the information in a logical way
- recognising bias
- deciding how to record the information
- reporting back to the class.

Children often work in groups as they go through the different stages of processing information

Directed activities related to text (DARTS)

DARTS are an important teaching tool in helping children read for information. They grow out of topic work in class and should not be used as isolated exercises. Teachers start with whole class discussion, then move to small group work. Finally each group reports back to the rest of the class. Activities include:

Cloze procedure

A passage with, say, every tenth word deleted encourages children to use their prior knowledge to fill the gaps.

Sequencing

Photocopied text is cut into sections for children to reassemble and justify the order they choose.

Modelling

Children underline the main points in a piece of writing and present these points in the form of a chart or diagram. They can then put the information to use in a wide variety of ways, such as designing a poster or writing a newspaper report.

A wide range of activities help children to understand and remember new information

Cloze procedure

Adopt-a-duck
Wild ducks travel far and wide during their life _____ and many duck adopters have enjoyed hearing of their _____ turning up somewhere in Europe, Scandinavia or even Russia.
_____ the years many thousands of ducks have been ringed _____ discover where they go on migration. One of the _____ long distance recoveries of an adopted duck was a _____ that reached Ekaterinaberg, in East Russia, 4,200 kilometres from _____ it was ringed.

Sequencing

Sniffles and snuffles and doses of flu,

and Hairy Maclary from Donaldson's Dairy.

Down at the Vet's there were all kinds of pets,

with troubles and woes from their ears to their toes.

So many animals watchful and wary,

Modelling

The Grand Canyon		
Where the traveller is	How old the rocks are	What fossils he finds
at the rim	200 million years	reptiles – lizards
half way down	400 million years	armoured fish bones
1 hour later	500 million years	shells, worms
three quarters of the way down	—	no sign of life
1 vertical mile down	2,000 million years	no organic remains

Children use many different skills to help them find the information they need

Library skills

By timetabling a regular weekly session in the school library, teachers can help children acquire the skills they need in the first stages of locating information:

- how books are classified
- how to find authors in alphabetical order
- how to use the 'blurb' on the cover to make decisions about book selection
- how to use a contents page and index when searching for something specific
- how to cope with the page layout in an encyclopaedia.

Parents can . . .
- encourage their children to join the local library and use it regularly
- remind them to use the index, contents page and headings when trying to find information for homework and projects
- remind them to keep in mind the particular piece of information they are looking for.

Parents in the classroom

Most teachers welcome help from parents. Another adult in the classroom can make a world of difference

The days when parents needed to make a formal appointment to speak to teachers are, thankfully, a thing of the past in the vast majority of schools. There is a much more informal relationship between parents and teachers, a recognition that school and home both have a vital part to play in children's education. The 1992 HMI report on reading went so far as to comment that strong and close parental support was associated with higher reading standards.

One example of the partnership between school and parents is the emergence of the home reading schemes that have sprung up all over the country. Very many teachers expect children to take books home to share with their parents or carers. Some schools provide a special notebook or a card and ask parents to make a note of their children's reactions to the book they read, or any problems they experience. This can be a very valuable channel of communication between school and home.

Throughout this book, we have pointed to things that parents can do to help their children at home. But most teachers will also welcome help in school from parents and other adults with time to spare.

Reading volunteers

Large numbers of schools welcome adult volunteers to hear children reading. Sometimes they take small groups of children; on other occasions they work with children on a one-to-one basis. In some schools, reading volunteers make it possible for children who are making slow progress to spend extra time on reading. In other schools, the volunteers are assigned to children making good progress with their reading, freeing the class teacher to work with children who have difficulties.

Strong and close parental support is associated with higher reading standards

Reading volunteers play a valuable part in many classrooms

Parents bring many different skills to the classroom

Making games and books

In some schools, parents take part in workshops to make reading games which can be used in school or at home. There have also been many successful projects where parents have written books about their own childhood, often illustrated by their children. Bilingual parents have been able to produce dual language books and games which can be enjoyed by all the children in the class.

Reading or taping stories

In classes where there are bilingual children, a good foundation in the language of the home is essential for future development in literacy. Parents can play a very valuable role in reading or telling stories either in person or on tape.

Monolingual English-speaking children also benefit by learning about other languages and the part they play in the community around them.

Working together in the classroom can be an enjoyable experience for parents and children alike

Working with children on the wordprocessor

An extra adult in the classroom can be very useful in helping children to 'publish' their stories.

The school bookshop

The bookshop is a popular feature of many schools. Sometimes it is run by teachers; sometimes by parents. Even when teachers are in charge, they will usually welcome offers of help from parents.

The school library

Teachers welcome assistance in running the library and also appreciate offers to repair and cover books.

Many parents enjoy regular visits to the school library to help their children choose new books.

Helping with the school bookshop is another way of sharing an interest in books

Assessing reading

The how and why of testing and the requirements of the National Curriculum

Teachers need to have a clear picture of which methods are working best

Children are assessed at the end of each Key Stage

Teachers assess children's work for a number of reasons. They need to have a clear picture of which methods are working best and which areas of the curriculum need more attention. It is also important to keep track of what children can and cannot do so that teachers can plan what they need to teach next.

Assessment of reading takes three main forms:
• standardised tests
• National Curriculum tests
• reading profiles.

Standardised tests

Even before the introduction of the National Curriculum, most local education authorities required schools to use standardised reading tests to assess children's reading performance, very often at the ages of seven, nine and eleven.

The spread of scores achieved by a large number of children on a particular test is used as a reference point to see whether they are above average, average or below average. If the average score of a child of seven years five months was 28, then all those children scoring 28 would be said to have a reading age of seven years five months.

Standardised tests have been widely criticised because:
• they often present an oversimplified view of reading
• they give little or no information on how the child sets about the task
• they do not help the teacher plan what to do next
• they offer little useful information about a child's progress over time
• there is inconsistency between tests. The same child can achieve very different scores on different standardised tests
• they are often culturally and linguistically biased.

National Curriculum tests

With the introduction of the National Curriculum, children will be assessed at the end of each Key Stage, at ages seven, eleven, fourteen and sixteen. The assessment of reading is based on a series of statements of attainment, divided into ten different levels. (See pages 39 and 40 for the statements of attainment for Levels 1 to 4).

Most seven year old children will be at Level 2; most eleven year olds are expected to have achieved Level 4. Children are said to have reached a Level when they have 'achieved' *all* the statements of attainment for that Level.

At the end of each Key Stage, children are asked to perform a number of standard assessment tasks (SATS). To achieve Level 2 at Key Stage 1, for instance, children are assessed as to whether they can read accurately and understand three of the signs or captions in the classroom. They are also asked to find a word in a dictionary during a writing activity or explain to a teacher how to use alphabetical order.

If they are successful, they are then allowed to read one of the books from the official booklist. When they reach a pre-selected passage, the teacher makes a 'running record' of each word that the child reads or attempts to read.

In deciding whether a child has achieved Level 2, a number of points have to be considered:

- teachers must tell the reader no more than eight words
- when a child makes incorrect attempts at words or 'miscues,' at least one must show an attempt to make sense of what is being read and at least one must show the use of phonics or word shape
- the child must be able to retell the gist of the passage and remember at least two of the main points
- the child must be able to make a sensible prediction about what might happen next
- a grade is also assigned for accuracy. A set number of words are highlighted in each passage. The teacher counts how many of these words are read correctly and translates this score into a grade.

At Level 2 of Key Stage 1, children need to show that they understand alphabetical order

Reading profiles

The information provided by National Curriculum testing is not nearly detailed enough to help teachers plan for individual children's progress. Well before the introduction of the National Curriculum, many schools had started keeping much broader reading profiles to record a child's performance throughout school life.

Teachers pay attention to a wide range of factors that affect children's development as readers, including:

- *attitudes* (enthusiasm for books; level of involvement in different reading activities; confidence in choosing books; favourite authors and illustrators, etc)
- *reading strategies* (reads word by word; goes for meaning, takes risks; self-corrects; uses initial letter cues, etc)
- *response to books* (savours language; responds to humour; relates stories to own experience; discusses characters, setting and plot, etc)
- *reading to learn* (finds way round library; uses card catalogues efficiently; uses dictionaries and thesauruses; selects important points, etc).

It is important to give as clear a picture as possible of children's reading preferences and reading habits in English and any other languages they may read. For this reason, a range of people in addition to the class teacher, including the children themselves and their parents, can contribute to the profile.

Name	John D.	Terms in school	1st
Date	Comment		Action
Sept	Thoroughly enjoys looking at books. Pores over pictures. Already knows how stories work.		Encourage him to predict what might happen next. Rhyming books might help.
Oct	Discovered Lynley Dodd's books and can't get enough of them! Getting 1-1 correspondence with words. Relates events to his own experiences.		Suggested he writes a letter to Lynley Dodd.

What to do if your child has a problem

Reasons for reading difficulties and ways to help

The rate of progress in learning to read varies enormously and some children simply need more time than others to become fluent readers. None the less, it can be very worrying when your own child does not seem to be progressing at the same rate as other members of the class.

There are many different reasons for reading difficulties and it is clearly very important to establish what lies at the root of the problem. In trying to identify the difficulty, you can call on a wide range of people for help – your doctor, the child's teacher and the various support services that work alongside the school.

Your own attitude is also very important. There are several dos and don'ts which apply to *all* parents trying to help their children learn to read.

It can be very worrying when your own child does not seem to be progressing at the same rate as other children in the class

Do...

- make reading enjoyable and carry on reading aloud to your children even when they have begun to read independently
- make sure that your child has lots of books to read
- praise your child's achievements, however small
- choose reading materials with care, remembering that:
  – books with refrains help visual memory
  – books should be within children's competence. It can be very frustrating to read a book that is too hard
  – books linked to children's hobbies and interests will improve motivation
  – humorous topics, e.g. books of jokes and riddles are likely to appeal to reluctant readers
- discuss any worries with your child's teacher who may be able to put your mind at rest and will certainly suggest ways that you can work together.

Don't...

- force children to take part in any activity against their will
- prolong an activity if the child is getting tired
- be concerned if your child keeps going back to the same book. It boosts confidence and guarantees success
- let your anxiety show if you are worried. Children are quick to pick up parental concern and this reduces their self-confidence still further
- expect miracles overnight. Reading is a complex process involving many different skills
- worry if *you* aren't a very confident reader. You can still enjoy looking at and talking about books with your child. You can also listen to tapes together.

Possible reasons for reading difficulties

Physical

Problem	Action
Hearing difficulties. Children may appear lost in a world of their own, offer disconnected answers or have unclear speech.	*Visit GP or request full screening from school medical service.*
Long sight, short sight, astigmatism, squint, excessive blinking. Children may screw up their eyes, struggle to focus, rub their eyes, have wobbly balance, frequent headaches, etc.	*Visit GP or request full screening from school medical service.*
Visual discomfort. When some people look at the printed page the words jump, change shape, wobble or go blurry. Colours sometimes come and go around the letters.	*Many children suffering from visual discomfort find that their reading speed and ability to focus is considerably improved when they use either colour tinted glasses or a coloured plastic overlay on the page. (See page 42 for details of the Irlen Centre).*
General ill health. Frequent absences from school can lead children to lose confidence in themselves as readers.	*If the school is not already doing so, ask the head or class teacher if it is possible for a volunteer helper, a member of staff or a specialist reading teacher to provide extra reading help.*

Emotional

Problem
Emotional trauma such as bereavement or divorce can cause children's progress to come to a halt
Poor self-image. Not making the same progress as friends may cause a child to adopt an attitude of 'see if I care' or 'reading is for wimps'.

Learning difficulties

	Action
	Explain what has happened to the school. All concerned can help children to come to terms with the loss by allowing them to grieve and talk about their feelings and perhaps share books that deal with the problem causing them distress (see Feelings *on page 41).*
	Keep showing the child how important reading is in your life. Keep reading to her so she understands that books can be enjoyable. Encourage her to use taped stories with books.

Problem	Action
Children who are late in learning to talk or who work with a speech therapist might well be delayed in their reading	*Keep talking and doing things together which encourage the child's general language development. If the school is not already doing so, ask the head or class teacher if it is possible for a volunteer helper, a member of staff or a specialist reading teacher to provide extra reading help.*
Some children are slow to develop in all areas of learning.	*In serious cases, it is possible to arrange a multiple professional assessment (MPA) to consider the best ways to help. This involves the child's teachers, an educational psychologist, the school doctor and the parents. The child may be entitled to support from a non-teaching assistant for a certain number of hours each week. A place in a school or unit for children with special educational needs may be offered, either on a part-time or a full-time basis.*
A child who experiences a range of difficulties related to print, e.g. reading, writing, spelling, left-right orientation, but not with any other school subjects is sometimes referred to as being 'dyslexic' or having 'specific learning difficulties'.	*An educational psychologist needs to make a very detailed and careful assessment of the child's needs. In severe cases, the headteacher will arrange an MPA and it may be possible to allocate a non-teaching assistant for a certain number of hours each week. The child will certainly need help from specialist teachers. Parents can also seek advice from the British Dyslexia Association or the Dyslexia Institute (see addresses on page 42).*

Reading Recovery is now being introduced into British schools

Reading Recovery Programme

You may well have seen reports in the press about a highly successful system developed by Dame Marie Clay in New Zealand. It sets out to identify reading difficulties when children reach their sixth birthday. This is in sharp contrast with the traditional British approach of allowing children to mature and waiting until they are over seven years old before offering specialist help.

The Reading Recovery Programme entails daily one-to-one sessions with a specially trained teacher over a period of weeks. Each session includes short periods of:

• reading a familiar book
• identifying letters
• analysing sounds in words
• making up and writing a story which is then cut up and re-sequenced
• discussing the next book that they will read.

The government is now committed to introducing the Reading Recovery Programme into British schools. It is unlikely that Reading Recovery on its own will be a cure-all for children with reading difficulties. However, it is a very welcome addition to the wide range of strategies which teachers already use to encourage children to become fluent readers.

Bilingualism and reading

There has been a great deal of confusion in the past about bilingualism. It has been blamed for all sorts of educational difficulties, including stammers and slow progress in reading. Because of this, teachers have sometimes advised parents to use only English in the home.

However, there is no evidence at all to support the idea that bilingualism is harmful. Bilingual children experience no more difficulty in learning to read than children who speak only English. On the contrary, recent research suggests that a sound foundation in the language of the home is essential for progress in English. The skills learned in one language are easily transferred to another.

Parents of bilingual children should encourage the use of home languages in the confidence that they are helping, not hindering, their children's educational development.

National curriculum statements of attainment for reading (Levels 1 to 4)

Level	Statements of attainment	Example
1	Pupils should be able to: **a)** recognise that print is used to carry meaning, in books and in other forms in the everyday world.	*Point to and recognise own name; tell the teacher that a label on a container says what is inside or that the words in a book tell a story.*
	b) begin to recognise individual words or letters in familiar contexts.	*In role-play, read simple signs such as shop names or brand names; recognise 'bus stop', 'exit', 'danger'.*
	c) show signs of a developing interest in reading.	*Pick up books and look at the pictures; choose books to hear or read.*
	d) talk in simple terms about the content of stories, or information in non-fiction books.	*Talk about characters and pictures, including likes and dislikes.*
2	**a)** read accurately and understand straightforward signs, labels and notices.	*Read labels on drawers in the classroom; read simple menus.*
	b) demonstrate knowledge of the alphabet in using word books and simple dictionaries.	*Turn towards the end to find words beginning with 's', rather than always starting from the beginning.*
	c) use picture and context cues, words recognise on sight and phonic cues in reading.	*Use a picture to help make sense of a text; recognise that 'Once' is often followed by 'upon a time'; use initial letters to help with recognising words.*
	d) describe what has happened in a story and predict what may happen next.	*Talk about how and why Jack climbs the beanstalk and suggest what may be at the top.*
	e) listen and respond to stories, poems and other material read aloud, expressing opinions informed by what has been read.	*Talk about the characters, their actions and appearance; discuss the behaviour of different animals described in a radio programme.*
	f) read a range of material with some independence, fluency, accuracy and understanding.	*Read something unprompted; talk with some confidence about what has been read; produce craftwork related to reading work.*

Level	Statements of attainment	Example
3	Pupils should be able to: **a)** read aloud from familiar stories and poems fluently and with appropriate expression.	*Raise or lower voice to indicate different characters.*
	b) read silently and with sustained concentration.	
	c) listen attentively to stories, talk about setting, story-line and characters and recall significant details.	*Talk about a story, saying what happened to change the fortunes of the leading characters.*
	d) demonstrate, in talking about stories and poems, that they are beginning to use inference, deduction and previous reading experience to find and appreciate meanings beyond the literal.	*Discuss what might happen to characters in a story, based on the outcome of adventures in other stories.*
	e) bring to their writing and discussion about stories some understanding of the way stories are structured.	*Refer to different parts of the story such as 'at the beginning' or 'the story ends with'; notice that some stories build up in a predictable way, e.g. 'The Three Little Pigs', 'Goldilocks and the Three Bears'.*
	f) devise a clear set of questions that will enable them to select and use appropriate information sources and reference books from the class and school library.	*Decide that the wildlife project needs information about the size and colour of birds, their food and habitat, and look it up.*
4	**a)** read aloud expressively, fluently and with increased confidence from a range of familiar literature.	*Vary the pace and tone of the voice to express feelings, or to represent character or mood.*
	b) demonstrate, in talking about a range of stories and poems which they have read, an ability to explore preferences.	*Describe those qualities of the poem or story which appeal and give an indication of personal response.*
	c) demonstrate, in talking about stories, poems, non-fiction and other texts, that they are developing their abilities to use inference, deduction and previous reading experience.	*Recognise and use those clues in a text which help the reader predict events.*
	d) find books or magazines in the class or school library by using the classification system, catalogue or database and use appropriate methods of finding information, when pursuing a line of inquiry.	*Use search reading to contribute to an inquiry into health and safety at school or in the home.*

Useful information on reading

Books

At Home in School: Parent Participation in Primary Schools
Viv Edwards and Angela Redfern (Routledge 1988)
ISBN 0415012945
A comprehensive survey of the ways parents can enter into partnership with schools, based on developments over time in an urban primary school.

Babies Need Books
Dorothy Butler (Penguin 1988)
ISBN 0140100946
A powerful plea from a grandmother and teacher for books to play a crucial role in children's lives from the very beginning.

The Early Detection of Reading Difficulties
Marie Clay (Heinemann 1986)
ISBN 0435802410
The methods outlined in this book form the basis for the Reading Recovery Programme.

Feelings
Cliff Moon (Reading and Language Information Centre 1992)
ISBN 0704905485
An annotated book list of recent children's paperbacks which explore issues such as death and ageing, friendship, fear, arguments, babies, growing up and loss.

Individualised Reading
Cliff Moon (Reading and Language Information Centre, updated annually)
Selected children's books covering the whole range required by the National Curriculum and graded into thirteen levels of difficulty. Originally intended for teachers, but it can also help parents choose books they know their child will be able to read. For instance, if your child is reading Book 6 from the *One, Two, Three and Away* reading scheme, this would be listed in Stage 8 of *Individualised Reading* which includes over 50 current paperbacks.

Learning to read at home: an assessment of guides for parents
Betty Root (Reading and Language Information Centre 1991)
An annotated list of guides for parents.

Well Read: sources of information on the teaching of reading in the primary school
Cliff Moon (Reading and Language Information Centre 1992)
ISBN 0704905493

Writing Partnerships (1): Home, School and Community. National Writing Project, National Curriculum Council/Nelson (1990)
ISBN 0174241208
Examples of projects involving the community that lives outside the school gates in the day-by-day writing activities of the children.

Magazines and newsletters

Bilingual Family Newsletter
Four issues a year from:
Multilingual Matters, Frankfurt Lodge, Clevedon Hall, Victoria Road, Clevedon, Avon BS21 7SJ (tel: 0275 876519)

Books for Keeps
Six issues a year from:
1 Effingham Road, Lee, London SE12 8NZ (tel: 081 852 4953)

Books for Your Children
Three issues a year from:
90 Gillhurst Road, Harborne, Birmingham 17 (tel: 021 454 5453)

Growing Point
Six issues a year from:
Ashton Manor, Ashton, Northants NN7 2JL

Book club

Letterbox Library
Unit 2D, Leroy House, 436 Essex Road, London N1 3QP (tel: 071 226 1633)
Non-sexist and multicultural selection of children's books

Organisations

The British Dyslexia Assocation
98 London Road, Reading, Berks RG1 5AU (tel: 0734 668271)

The Dyslexia Institute
133 Gresham Road, Staines, Middlesex TW18 2AJ (0784 463851)

The Children's Book Foundation
Book Trust, 45 East Hill, London SW18 2QZ (tel: 081 870 9055)

The Irlen Centre
4 Moscow Mansions, 224 Cromwell Road, London SW5 0SP (tel: 071 244 7099)
Suppliers of coloured overlays for children experiencing reading discomfort

The National Library for the Handicapped Child
Ash Court, Rose Street, Wokingham, Berks (tel: 0734 891101)

The Reading and Language Information Centre,
University of Reading, Bulmershe Court, Earley, Reading RG6 1HY (tel: 0734 318820)
In addition to publications for teachers, the Reading and Language Information Centre produce a wide range of pamphlets for parents:

- *Books to share at home with children aged 0–3 years*
- *Books to share at home with children aged 3–5 years*
- *Books to share at home with children aged 5–7 years*
- *Books for the 7–9 year old who is finding reading difficult*
- *Books for the 7–9 year old who is bored with reading*
- *Books for the keen reader of 7–9 years*
- *Preparing your child for reading. Advice for parents of 2–5 year olds*
- *How to help your child with reading. Advice for parents of children 4– 7 years*
- *How to help your child with writing. Advice for parents of children 3–7 years*
- *Helping children with reading*
- *Helping children with spelling*
- *Children with reading difficulties*
- *Alphabet books.*

Index